☛ Three *More* Tenners ☚

Three ten-minute youth plays

"Don't Let Bigfoot Bite!"

"Money in the Graveyard"

and

"Katie and the Crutches"

by
John Glass

john@studentplays.org

Copyright information. Please read!

These plays have full protection under the copyright rules of the United States. No one may produce these plays without written permission of *Student Plays*. Unless otherwise told by *Student Plays*, you must pay a royalty every time these plays are produced in front of a live audience.

You may not copy any part of these plays without written permission.

Please give credit to the author and to *Student Plays* on all printed programs when producing these plays.

Please respect the work of the playwrights at *Student Plays*! Violating copyright law is a serious offense. If you are unsure or have any questions please contact us at john@studentplays.org or at 251-463-8650.

☞ About Student Plays ☜

Student Plays consists of **John Glass, Jackie Jernigan,** and **Dominic Torres.** We are a group of playwrights and directors that have written scripts for elementary school through college. We are proud of the variety of ages that our scripts serve.

Student Plays has "creepy" plays, and we also have Latino-themed plays. These are scripts that focus on Latino youths and the Latino experience. Any school can perform a Latino-themed play: it just requires a general introduction and basic exposure to the Spanish language, something that most schools and students already have.

To contact *Student Plays* or to communicate with one of the playwrights, simply email us at john@studentplays.org.

Money in the Graveyard

\-

A ten-minute play

by
John Glass

☞   ☞

Money in the Graveyard

MOLLY   Not scared of woods. Wants to find money!

GARY   Not scared of woods. Wants to find money!

BOBBY   Prankster.

LEXI   Prankster.

McKENNA   Very scared of the woods.

AVA   Adventurous.

EMMA   Adventurous.

MIGUEL   Very scared of the woods.

This play is written for **grades 5-8**. The time is the present, the setting a school and a nearby graveyard.

Scene One takes place at a school. **Scene Two** takes place in the graveyard. **Scene Three** takes place back at the school.

Needs: flashlights, pine straw, tree branches, gravestones (optional), a large bag of counterfeit money, small shovels/spades, old books, a yellowed map and backpacks.

The gender for all of the roles can easily be swapped for the opposite gender. Students of any gender can perform any of the roles. Simply change the name to match the gender.

At RISE: MOLLY and GARY are just joining BOBBY and LEXI, who are looking over several old books. The students are all at school, about to go to class.

MOLLY: Okay, so tell us. What did you guys want to show us?

GARY: Yeah! And what are these old books?

BOBBY: I told you. My grandma loves garage sales.

LEXI: Yes she does . . .

BOBBY: I went last weekend with her and bought these.

LEXI: Trash!

MOLLY: It's not trash. These are cool, Bobby. I like them.

GARY: You *would* like them.

MOLLY: Be quiet. *(To BOBBY.)* So is that it? What else??

BOBBY: *(Pulling a map out from a book.)* Well . . . here's what I really want to show you guys.

GARY: What is that? A map?

BOBBY: Yep. My grandma found it in these old books.

MOLLY: Cool!

LEXI: *(Pointing.)* Look where it leads to . . .

GARY: Where . . .?

BOBBY: The Jonestown Cemetery.

MOLLY: The cemetery??

GARY: *(Humorously.)* Ohhh!! The Jonestown Cemetary!

BOBBY: There's a big x right here.

MOLLY: Cool. Let's go!

LEXI: Not cool. I'm not going out there.

BOBBY: Neither am I. Creepy! Here, take it.
    (Passes the map to them.)

MOLLY: Well, heck. *I'll* go!

GARY: I'll go with you!

MOLLY: Good. How about tonight?

LEXI: Tonight?

MOLLY: Sure. Let's do it tonight. You guys don't wanna come?

BOBBY: Not me. All those pine trees! This is the Jonestown Cemetery. The Pine Ghost lives out there. *You* know the legend!

MOLLY: Quit. There *is* no Pine Ghost. Bobby, this is *your* map. Come on . . . it'll be fun!

BOBBY: No, keep it. That cemetery is creepy!

LEXI: Yes it is! You guys are crazy!

GARY: Molly, we can get Emma and Ava and their sisters to go with us.

MOLLY: Yeah, good idea!

BOBBY: *Those* girls . . ? Hmmmpph.

LEXI: Guys, are you sure about this??

MOLLY: Yes! There might be money there!

BOBBY: Well, *maybe* . . .

LEXI: Money?? Whatever! I doubt it!

BOBBY: There *might* be money. But I'm not going out there!

MOLLY: Dinero!

GARY: Money!

MOLLY: Cash! Dinero en el graveyard!

BOBBY: Huh . . . ?

MOLLY: Dinero en el graveyard! You know, *money in the graveyard!*

GARY: Yep!

LEXI: All right, enough of this nonsense. We have drum class. Let's go, Bobby.

> *(They all begin to exit. BOBBY and LEXI leave together, MOLLY and GARY leave together.)*

GARY: And *we* have history. Later!

BOBBY: Have fun this weekend! In the cemetery!! With the *Pine Ghost!*

MOLLY: When we find that money, I'll accept your apology.

GARY: Hah!

BOBBY: Please! There's no money out there!

LEXI: Later, guys!

MOLLY: Bye!

(Everybody exits. End of scene.)

SCENE TWO

The local cemetery. Except for BOBBY and LEXI, the entire cast enters, slowly and quietly.

MIGUEL: Wow . . .

McKENNA: This is scary!

AVA: This is cool!

EMMA: Ssshh!!

MOLLY: What? Nobody's out here!

McKENNA: What about the Pine Ghost?

MIGUEL: Yeah!

GARY: Hush. There is no Pine Ghost.

McKENNA: How do you know? Look at all these pine trees!

EMMA: Oh, stop it.

MOLLY: Yeah. I thought you guys were brave.

AVA: Molly, do you have the map?

MOLLY: Right here.

EMMA: Great. Let's have a look!

McKENNA: Why is that tree branch moving?

GARY: Hush! That's the wind.

MIGUEL: Are you sure?

AVA: Yes, we're sure!!

McKENNA: Do you know why he's called the Pine Ghost?

MOLLY: Why?

MIGUEL: Because he lives in the pine trees!!

MOLLY: Guys, quit! *(Looking at the map.)* Okay . . . let's have a look. Hmmm. The X is by two graves.

EMMA: Well . . . here are the two graves.

GARY: *(Looking at map.)* And it's also by the pine trees.

AVA: Here are the pine trees.

McKENNA: Don't remind me!!

GARY: Stop! Come on! Help us look . . . *(Looking at map)*

MOLLY: It shows the X is right here . . . right by the second grave.

EMMA: Yep. *(Pointing at map.)* There it is.

MOLLY: Okay. Let's dig!

(AVA and EMMA begin to dig.)

McKENNA: Right here?

MOLLY: Yes! X marks the spot, silly.

MIGUEL: All right! Get to it, you two! Start digging.

GARY: *(Singing)* "Money in the Graveyard . .!"

EMMA: Great. Maybe your singing will scare away the Pine Ghost.

MOLLY: There *is* no Pine Ghost. Come on. Dig!

EMMA: We are!

MIGUEL: Yeah!

McKENNA: *(Hearing something.)* Umm . . what is *that?*

AVA: *(Discovering something in the hole.)* Umm . . . what is *that*?

(Everyone except for McKENNA and MIGUEL stares down into the hole, curious. McKENNA is scared of what she heard.)

GARY: What is it . .?

McKENNA: *(Staring off into woods.)* Did you guys hear that . . ?

EMMA: A bag!

McKENNA: Ummm . . . guys?

GARY: A *what*?

EMMA: A bag! A bag of money!

AVA: Come on . . . help me grab it.

(MOLLY, AVA, and EMMA all carefully lift the bag. There are stacks of money falling out of the top of the bag.)

McKENNA: I heard something!

MIGUEL: So did I!

MOLLY: It's heavy!

McKENNA: Guys! It's the Pine Ghost!

GARY: McKenna, stop!

MIGUEL: It's true!

AVA: Look at all this money!!

McKENNA: We should go . . !

EMMA: Molly, you guys were right! It's money!

GARY: Lots of it!

AVA: We can retire!

MOLLY: What do you mean, *we*? This was our idea!!

GARY: Well, there's enough to go around! We're rich!

MOLLY: *(Grabbing the money, begins to exit.)* Come on! Let's get out of here!

AVA: Let's go!

McKENNA: This place freaks me out!

MIGUEL: You got that right!

EMMA: Oh, be quiet!

AVA: Yeah, *everything* freaks you two out!

　　　　(They exit in a hurry. End of scene.)

SCENE THREE

*Monday morning, at school. BOBBY and LEXI are
standing, looking at a notebook/papers for class.
Enter GARY and MOLLY, who promptly walk over to
them.*

GARY: Well, well, well . . . look what the cat dragged
in!

BOBBY: Oh. Hi!

LEXI: Um . . buenos días!

MOLLY: Buenos días to *you!* Have a good weekend?

BOBBY: Uh . . what?

GARY: Did you guys have a good weekend?

LEXI: Yeah.

BOBBY: I guess so. How about you guys?

GARY: Oh, sure.

MOLLY: It was wonderful.

GARY: Great.

MOLLY: Fantastic.

(BOBBY and LEXI nervously attempt to leave.)

BOBBY: Okay, well, we have class now.

LEXI: Yep!

MOLLY: *(Grabs his arm.)* Not. So. Fast!

LEXI: Uh . . what's wrong?

MOLLY: What's wrong? What's wrong?? *(Pulls out a handful of fake money.)* Does *this* look familiar?

BOBBY: Oh! You found the money!

LEXI: Super!

GARY: Not super! This money is fake!

BOBBY: What?

MOLLY: And you guys know it!

GARY: Drop the act! You two buried this fake money in the graveyard!

LEXI: *(To BOBBY.)* Ughh! See?? I told you she'd be upset!

BOBBY: Oh, guys . . . we are sorry!

LEXI: So sorry!!

BOBBY: Please forgive us! We thought it would be funny!

GARY: Funny? We were in a *graveyard*!!

MOLLY: In the middle of the night!

GARY: On a wild goose chase!!

BOBBY: *(Sadly.)* I know . . . .

LEXI: *(To BOBBY.)* I told you it was a bad idea!

BOBBY: You never told me that!

LEXI: Yes I did!

MOLLY: Whatever. Okay, here is what we want . .

LEXI: What is it?

MOLLY: You two are going to carry our backpacks.

BOBBY: Your . . . backpacks?

GARY: Yes. All week. Beginning *now*!

LEXI: Now??

MOLLY: Yep.

BOBBY: Um . . . okay.

LEXI: Okay. That's only fair. I guess.

MOLLY: You can carry them from class to class. Get our backpacks, Gary.

> *(MOLLY turns to face the backpacks as GARY goes to get them. BOBBY and LEXI try to sneak away as her back is turned.)*

GARY*:* Backpacks on the way!

MOLLY: Yep! I'm going to enjoy this. *(Turns to see them running away.)* Hey! Wait a minute!!

BOBBY: Later, guys!

LEXI: Gotta go!

> *(AVA and EMMA abruptly enter, blocking their exit.)*

AVA: Excuse me . . . ?

EMMA: Going somewhere??

LEXI: Ohhh!

BOBBY: Aghhh!

> *(They run to the other side of the stage and try to exit. Enter MIGUEL and McKENNA, who abruptly block their exit.)*

MIGUEL: Hello?!?

McKENNA: Going somewhere??

BOBBY: Agghh!

LEXI: No!!

(They turn to see GARY holding out the backpacks; they face the audience and crumble to the ground as GARY drops the backpacks on top of them.)

BOBBY & LEXI: Agggghhhh!

(Lights fade. End of play.)

Don't Let Bigfoot Bite!

-

A ten-minute play

by

John Glass

☞   ☞

Don't Let Bigfoot Bite!

ALAINA   Camper. Scared of Bigfoot.

TEDDY   Camper. Scared of Bigfoot.

AVA   Camper. Scared of Bigfoot.

ISABELLA   Camper. <u>Does not</u> believe in Bigfoot.

KEN   Camper. <u>Does not</u> believe in Bigfoot.

VALENTINA   Park Ranger.

DYLAN   Park Ranger.

This play is written for <u>grades 5-8</u>. The campers are camping out in a state park and are about to go to bed. The park rangers are talking to them. There are sleeping bags on the ground, pillows, etc. A small fire is nearby.

Needs: a small campfire, a large set of dried footprints, flashlights, sleeping bags, pajamas, park ranger shirts/badges/hats, cell phone, pine straw, pinecones, twigs, etc.

The gender for all of the roles can easily be swapped for the opposite gender. Students of any gender can perform any of the roles. Simply change the name to match the gender.

(At RISE: As the lights go up, a loud, eerie noise is heard from the forest.)

ALAINA: See? Don't you hear that?

VALENTINA: It's a wolf.

ALAINA: It's not a wolf! Wolves don't sound like that!!

AVA: Right!

VALENTINA: Look, calm down. Okay? There's no Bigfoot in these woods. That sound was a wolf.

TEDDY: Hmmmph.

DYLAN: Guys, Bigfoot doesn't exist.

VALENTINA: It's probably your friend out there, in the other campground.

ISABELLA: That's what I told them!

TEDDY: *(Holding up a dried, muddy footprint.)* Then how do you explain this footprint??

VALENTINA: Anybody could do that!

ISABELLA: Anybody!!

TEDDY: Are you sure?? Look how big this thing is!

VALENTINA: Yes, I'm sure! This was just a trick!

DYLAN: Your friend probably did that. With some big wooden feet. Where is your friend, anyway?

AVA: *(Pointing off to the woods.)* Over there. In campground number 4.

TEDDY: *(To the rangers.)* Yeah, his name is Jimmy. His family didn't want to camp with us.

DYLAN: Oh. Okay.

AVA: Yeah, they're kind of weird.

VALENTINA: Well . . . . Jimmy's probably the one that's doing it. That's all.
    (Begins to leave.)
And look, we have to go. We have to go check on a pack of wild raccoons in campsite number one.

ALAINA: Okay . . .

VALENTINA: Remember, guys . . . . that sound was a wolf.

AVA: If you say so . . .

DYLAN: There *is* no Bigfoot. We promise.

VALENTINA: You guys get some sleep, okay? It's late. We need to go.

DYLAN: Yeah, these raccoons are waiting for us.

VALENTINA: Good night.

TEDDY: Bye.

ISABELLA: Bye.

KEN: Later.

(VALENTINA and DYLAN exit.)

ISABELLA: See? I told you there was no Bigfoot out here!

KEN: Yeah, it's just Jimmy and his family, playing a joke. You know how Jimmy is.

ALAINA: But I don't know . . . how would he make that sound?

ISABELLA: Who knows? Maybe his dad has a horn or something.

KEN: His dad has all kinds of weird things in his garage.

ALAINA: Whatever.

AVA: Well . . . come on, we had a long day. It's bedtime.

(They begin to turn in.)

TEDDY: I am beat!

KEN: Me too.

ALAINA: But what about Bigfoot??

ISABELLA: There is no Bigfoot! He doesn't exist!

AVA: I'm not so sure . . . !

ALAINA: Ohhhh . . .!

ISABELLA: Come on, guys. It's bedtime.

KEN: Yeah, I'm tired. We can talk about large, hairy creatures that *don't exist* in the morning.

ALAINA: *(Sighing.)* Good night . . .

AVA: Good night.

TEDDY: Night night . . sleep tight . . .

ISABELLA & KEN: Don't let Bigfoot bite!

ALAINA: Don't do that!!

ISABELLA: *(Evil cackle.)* Ha ha . . . sorry!

> *(They close their eyes and try to go to sleep. Long pause. An owl is heard.)*

ALAINA: What is that??

ISABELLA: What??

ALAINA: That sound!!

KEN: An owl.

ALAINA: What?

ISABELLA: It's an owl!

KEN: Yeah. Don't you know what an owl sounds like??

ALAINA: Ohhh . . !

(Pause. The hooting is heard again.)

ALAINA: There is it again!!

KEN: It's an owl!!

ALAINA: Are you sure??

ISABELLA: Go to sleep, Alaina!!

KEN: Yeah!!

ALAINA: Ohhh!!!

(Long pause. The eerie noise is heard from the woods again.)

ALAINA: What is that??

ISABELLA: Probably a small animal. A rabbit. Maybe a squirrel.

ALAINA: How do you know??

KEN: Go to sleep! Good grief!!

ALAINA: TEDDY!! AVA! Aren't you guys scared too? *(Pause.)* Guys???

ISABELLA: They're sleeping.

KEN: They're sound asleep. You should be asleep too.

ALAINA: Ohhhh! Whatever.

ISABELLA: I knew we shouldn't have brought you camping.

ALAINA: Huh??

KEN: It's true! You are ruining the whole trip!

ISABELLA: It's true!! Now go to sleep!

> *(Long pause. The eerie noise in the woods is heard again.)*

ALAINA: There it is!!

KEN: It's just a squirrel or something! We told you. *(Beat.)* Why did you come camping with us??

ISABELLA: Yeah, why??

ALAINA: Sorry.

ISABELLA: You are scared of everything!!

KEN: Yep.

ISABELLA: And you are ruining our camping trip!! *(Pause.)* Now, please . . . . can we go to sleep?

ALAINA: Yes.

ISABELLA: Thank you!!

(Long pause. ALAINA feels bad.)

ALAINA: Guys . . ? Um, still awake?

KEN: Yes!!

ISABELLA: What is it, Alaina??

ALAINA: Guys, I'm sorry. Please forgive me. Oh, please forgive me! It's true, I *am* scared of everything. I came on this trip to get over being scared. And . . . well . . . I'm not doing a great job.

KEN: It's okay.

ISABELLA: Yeah. You'll get there. I know it's hard. I used to be scared of the woods all the time. But now I love it out here.

ALAINA: I know you do.

ISABELLA: You'll get there.

KEN: Yeah.

ALAINA: Well, thanks a lot. That means a lot to me. I know there's no Bigfoot out there . . . but I just get scared sometimes.

KEN: It's okay.

ISABELLA: It's fine.

ALAINA: Well, I appreciate it. *(Pause.)* Okay! Now I feel better. Good night!

KEN: Good night.

ISABELLA: 'Night.

(Long pause. The eerie noise is heard again.)

ALAINA: Um . . . . it's just an owl, right?

KEN: Yep. Just an owl or something.

(The eerie noise is heard again.)

ALAINA: *(Becoming more scared.)* Yep. Only an owl.

ISABELLA: That's right. *(Beat. Sits up and looks at her cell phone.)* Oh, what is this? My phone . . .

KEN: Huh?

ISABELLA: I got a text.

KEN: What?? You brought your phone out here??

ISABELLA: Yes.

KEN: Brother . . .

ISABELLA: My parents made me. In case I had to call them. *(Reading the text.)* Um . . . guys?

ALAINA: What?

ISABELLA: It's from Jimmy's mom.

KEN: Well . . . ? What does she say?

TEDDY: *(Waking up, yawning.)* Are you guys *ever* going to sleep??

AVA: *(Also waking up.)* Yeah!!

TEDDY: Man!

ISABELLA: *(Still reading.)* Oh no!

ALAINA: What?

ISABELLA: She says that they left!!

AVA: What??

ISABELLA: Jimmy's family left the campsite! His dad got sick and they had to leave!! They left an hour ago!!

KEN: Oh. So . . . if they left . . then who is making those noises??

ISABELLA: Um . . .

TEDDY: Um . . .

ALAINA: Um . . .

EVERYBODY: BIGFOOT!

(They all scramble to get up.)

ISABELLA: Let's go!

ALAINA: Come on!

AVA: Let's get outta here!!

ALAINA: I *told* you guys!!

ISABELLA: Oh, be quiet!

ALAINA: I did tell you!

TEDDY: No, *we* told them!

ALAINA: I want an apology!!

>   *(Enter DYLAN and VALENTINA, terrified, out of breath.)*

KEN: And *I* want to live! Come on!

ISABELLA: Run!

DYLAN: Hey campers!

KEN: What??

VALENTINA: Guess who we just saw??

ALAINA: We're way ahead of you!

>   *(The eerie noise is heard again.)*

EVERYBODY: Agghhhhh!!!

>   *(They all exit in a scramble, screaming, running, etc. End of play.)*

Katie and the Crutches

-

A ten-minute play

by
John Glass

☞ ☞

Katie and the Crutches

KATIE   Bossy. Throughout the play, Katie is faking an injury.

STEVE   Exhausted from working.

KRYSTA   Exhausted from working.

LILY   Exhausted from working.

ALAINA   Exhausted from working.

This play is written for <u>grades 5 through 8.</u> The time is the present, the setting is the living room in Katie's house. The characters are all friends.

Needs: one pair of crutches, several brooms and dustpans, a duster, other typical household cleaning tools, a food tray with various food items.

The gender for all of the roles can easily be swapped for the opposite gender. Students of any gender can perform any of the roles. Simply change the name to match the gender.

(At RISE: As the lights go up, KATIE is on her crutches, standing, in pain from a leg injury. She is on the phone with her Aunt Charlotte. STEVE and LILY are doing various chores in the room, sweeping, cleaning, etc.)

KATIE: No, it's fine, aunt Charlotte.
        (Pause.)
Yes! I'll be fine. I have my friends here to help me.
        (Pause.)
Yes. I know!!
        (Pause.)
Okay, thanks. I will. Bye, aunt Charlotte. Thank you. And don't you worry about a thing!! My friends are here! Bye!

        (She hangs up. Pause as she winces in pain.)

STEVE: What did she say?

KATIE: I told her not to come over.

LILY: Why?

KATIE: Because you guys are here, helping me. Besides, my aunt is busy.

STEVE: Well . . . what about your parents?

KATIE: I talked to them earlier. They're coming home Wednesday night.

LILY: Wednesday . . . ?

STEVE: *Night . . . ?*

KATIE: Yes. They couldn't get an earlier flight back from Chicago.

LILY: Wow. That's two days away.

KATIE: I know . . . *(In pain.)* Ohhh!! *(She sits down.)*

STEVE: Your leg still hurts, huh?

KATIE: Yes! Of course!

STEVE: Well, what did the doctor say? You never told us.

KATIE: He said I'll need these crutches for three weeks!

LILY: Three weeks?

STEVE: That's a long time. Katie, we feel so bad about this.

KATIE: Well, you should! I told you I didn't want to play that dumb wrestling game!

LILY: It was an accident.

STEVE: Yeah.

KATIE: I still told you guys. *(Wincing.)* Ohhh!!

LILY: Well . . . are you going to need any more help around the house?

KATIE: Absolutely!

LILY: Absolutely . . ?

KATIE: Yes. There's a lot to do. It's my parents' anniversary. And I need everything to be clean when they get home.

STEVE: Uh . . . everything?

KATIE: Yep. There's lots to do. The kitchen. The bathroom.

LILY: The *bathroom?*

KATIE: Yep. It's only fair, right? You guys forced me into that game . . . and I got hurt . . . right?

LILY: Um. Right.

STEVE: Right. Sort of.

KATIE: And also, I need your help. I can't make my lunch! My dinner!

LILY: But we've been here all morning! Working!

KATIE: Well, it's okay. I have Krysta and Alaina here to help me too. For now.

STEVE: *(Relieved.)* Yes you do!

KATIE: But I will still need you guys later on today.

LILY: Later on . . ?

STEVE: *Today . . ?*

KATIE: Yep. And tomorrow too.

STEVE: What?? Tomorrow?

> *(Enter KRYSTA and ALAINA, carrying food on a tray. They are tired from working.)*

KATIE: Yes. My parents don't get back until Wednesday night. So there's work to be done. And I obviously can't do it!

KRYSTA: Here we go . . . lunchtime.

KATIE: Ahh, perfect! Did you make soup?

ALAINA: Yes.

KATIE: With bread?

KRYSTA: Yes . . .

KATIE: Crackers?

ALAINA: Yes. We have everything.

KATIE: Excellent. You can put it right there on the table.

LILY: Okay, is there anything else, Katie?

STEVE: Yeah, we're tired! We're ready to go!

KATIE: I think you guys can go. Alaina and Krysta are here so they can help me.

KRYSTA: Huh?

ALAINA: Still . . ?

KATIE: Yep. *(Pointing to LILY and STEVE.)* And you two can go. But come back later!

> *(STEVE and LILY hurriedly and eagerly begin to exit.)*

STEVE: Okay. Have fun, you guys.

LILY: Yeah!

STEVE: Adiós!!

ALAINA: Later.

KATIE: See you guys in a few hours.

>   *(They exit in a hurry. KATE begins to stir the soup.)*

KATIE: Ahhh. This is nice. But, ohh . . . my leg.

ALAINA: Again?? More pain?

KATIE: Yes. Could you please put that pillow under my foot?

KRYSTA: Yes. *(Grabs a pillow and does so.)*

KATIE: That would be nice. Thanks.

KRYSTA: Here you go.

KATIE: Careful!

KRYSTA: I am!

KATIE: *(Helping her arrange the pillow.)* Okay, right there. Much better.
>   *(Beat.)*
Now . . . I need one of you to sweep the back patio.

KRYSTA: What??

KATIE: The patio. You know. I want it to be clean when my parents arrive.

ALAINA: The patio is full of leaves! Thousands of them!

KATIE: Exactly! And it's obvious that I can't do it . . . right?

KRYSTA: Well . . .

KATIE: Right?

ALAINA: Right. I guess so . . .

KATIE: Good. So, the broom is already on the patio. Alaina, you can begin now. Krysta can bag them up when you're done.

ALAINA: *(Grudgingly begins to exit.)* Oh. Okay.

KATIE: Chop-chop!

ALAINA: I'm going!! I'm going!!

    (She exits quickly.)

KATIE: Good. Okay, that's taken care of. Now . . . where was I?

KRYSTA: You were about to eat your soup.

KATIE: Right! My soup. Okay, here we go . . .

(She begins to eat her soup. KRYSTA tries to exit, slowly.)

KATIE: Mmmmm. Boy, this is good. Really, really good. *(Beat. Sees KRYSTA leaving.)* Um, excuse me?? Are you leaving?

KRYSTA: Ummm, yes! I just wanted to get a snack for myself.

KATIE: Well, I could use some juice.

KRYSTA: Juice?

KATIE: Yes. Please?

KRYSTA: Oh, okay.

KATIE: Thanks. And there are some cookies in the kitchen. Bring those.

KRYSTA: Cookies?? And juice??

KATIE: I'm hungry! And I'm in pain!

KRYSTA: Sorry! Okay!

KATIE: The doctor said food will distract the pain! I have to obey his orders!

KRYSTA: *(Exiting.)* I'm going, I'm going!

KATIE: Thank you! And don't forget that you have to help Alaina after you bring me that.

KRYSTA: Good grief! I know!

(KRYSTA exits. After a moment, KATIE looks around, then tosses the crutches to the side. She stands and begins to walk around freely, doing a jig as she speaks.)

KATIE: Ahhh! Life is pretty good. My lunch is made! My dinner will be made! The patio is being swept. The house is being cleaned. Ha! I'll have to get hurt more often!

(Pause. She sits back down, sips more of her soup, then sits back and relaxes, closing her eyes)

Yes. I'll have to get hurt more often. I really will!

(Long pause. Her eyes remain closed and the lights fade to black. Here, to indicate a quick scene break, there can be a simple music cue. After a few seconds, the lights quickly come back up. KATIE is still seated, now napping. Enter STEVE, LILY, and KRYSTA. They are weary from all of the work. KATIE hears them

and sits up abruptly. She is very animated here, exaggerating her appreciation.)

KATIE: Well . . . hello!

STEVE: We finished the work. It took forever!

KATIE: Wow. All of it?

LILY: Yes. The bedrooms.

KATIE: Super!

KRYSTA: The bathroom.

KATIE: Spectacular!

STEVE: The dining room.

KATIE: *(Singing.)* "The dining room, the—"

LILY: Will you stop??

KATIE: What?? What did I do??

LILY: We are exhausted, Katie. We're your friends. But we've done a lot of work!

KRYSTA: Tell me about it!

(Enter ALAINA, exhausted, holding a plate with a piece of cherry pie.)

STEVE: Vacuuming, sweeping, scrubbing! Your bedroom was disgusting!

KRYSTA: Yes. It. Was.

KATIE: Well, I *am* hurt, you know.

ALAINA: And *I* am hungry.

KATIE: Excuse me?

ALAINA: I'm going to sit down right here and eat this.

KATIE: Is that my cherry pie?

KRYSTA: Uh, your last piece of cherry pie.

KATIE: What??

LILY: I ate the second-to-last piece!

ALAINA: Sorry but this girl needs food. I swept the whole patio. And I raked the yard.

KATIE: I was going to eat that!

ALAINA: Oh well. I'm hungry!

(She raises her fork to eat when KATIE jumps up and runs over, grabs the plate from her.)

KATIE: Stop! I told you! That is *my* pie!

ALAINA: Ohhhh!

KATIE: Not *yours!!*

(Pause. Everybody stares at her and gasps, in total shock.)

ALAINA: Uhhh . . .

STEVE: What??

KRYSTA: You . . . can walk?

KATIE: Ohh!! Well, hallelulah! That medicine sure did work!

ALAINA: I can't believe it!

KATIE: Neither can I! What a miracle!

LILY: Katie, cut the comedy!

STEVE: Yeah! You were lying to us!

KATIE: No!

KRYSTA: How could you . . . ?

ALAINA: *(With disdain.)* I don't even know you anymore!

LILY: Neither do I!

KATIE: *(Drops to her knees)* Oh, guys, please, please, please forgive me!

STEVE: Why should we?

KATIE: I just found out my leg was okay!

LILY: What?

KATIE: Seriously! The doctor called and told me! While you guys were outside working!!

LILY: But were you going to tell us??

KATIE: Yes!

KRYSTA: Are you sure?

KATIE: Yes!

ALAINA: But you just said that you were still hurt! You weren't going to tell us!

(They all advance towards her.)

LILY: Tell the truth, woman! You didn't get hurt in that wrestling game!

STEVE: Yeah! You made us do all that work!

KATIE: No, wait!!

LILY: Let's get her!

KRYSTA: Hold her down!

KATIE: Guys, WAIT!!

(They come to a stop. Pause.)

KATIE: Look, I'm sorry that I lied to you. I'll make it up to you. I promise!

ALAINA: How?

KATIE: I'm come and clean your bedrooms.

LILY: Really?

KATIE: And your bathrooms.

STEVE: Really?

KATIE: And your kitchens!

KRYSTA: Really?

ALAINA: What about the leaves in our yards?

KATIE: I'll rake them!

LILY: I've got a big backyard.

STEVE: And I've got a messy bedroom.

KATIE: I'll do it. All of it!

STEVE: When??

KATIE: I'll get started right now! Come on let's go!

(They begin to exit.)

LILY: Okay . . . but my house is first!

ALAINA: No, *my* house is first!

STEVE: No, *my* house is first!

(In their haste KATIE falls down.)

KRYSTA: Be careful!

KATIE: Aghh! Oh!

ALAINA: Oh no.

KATIE: Oh, my leg!

LILY: Are you okay?

KATIE: *(In great pain.)* Ohhh!!!

STEVE: I can't believe this!

KRYSTA: Neither can I!!

KATIE: Guys . . . ?

LILY: What??

ALAINA: Don't tell me . . .

KRYSTA: Please don't tell me . . !

KATIE: My leg really is hurt!!!

> *(Everybody except for KATIE turns to the audience at the same time.)*

STEVE, LILY, ALAINA & KRYSTA: NOT AGAIN!!

> *(They all turn back to her, groaning and staring. Lights fade to black. End of play.)*

☞ **More from Student Plays** ☜

Othello's Just Another Fellow

Dramedy. **Grades 5-7.** 25-35 minutes. 8 actors: 4 males, 3 females, one teacher (or student portraying a teacher) 3 to 5 extras, if needed. ****A Latino-themed play****

A group of students are involved in a school production of *Othello*, but one of them is disturbed about the lack of diversity in the play. He takes certain steps to disrupt the play but in the end is encouraged by the others to try and make a difference in another, more constructive way. A lesson is learned, and the production is saved from disaster!

Pagasqueeny's Pantry

Comedy. **Middle/High School.** 15-20 minutes. 6 actors: 3 females, 2 males. One student (or a teacher) plays the comical role of the elderly Mr. Pagasqueeny.

Three friends sneak into Mr. Pagasqueeny's home to get something that one of them left behind. But in walks Pagasqueeny and they must hide in the pantry! In this comical play, a lesson is learned about honesty and trust, but it takes a heated discussion in the pantry and a subsequent attempt to escape to find this out!

Una Carta de Abuelo

Dramedy. **Middle/High School.** 35-45 minutes. 10 actors: 1 teacher, 5 females, 4 males. (With the option of 4-5 extra actors in two scenes.)   ****A Latino-themed play****

Two cousins discover an old letter in their late grandfather's comic collection that they think leads to treasure! The cousins often butt heads, with one believing that he is more "Mexican," the other believing that some people make too much of a fuss about "being Mexican." Thus, they form their *own* groups in search of what Grandpa hid long ago. But what they find is actually worth more than merely silver or gold.

Barbecue at the Prom!

Dramedy. **Grades 5-8.** 25-35 minutes. 6 actors: 3 females, 3 males

It's a classic tale of guys versus girls! It's a prom committee, and everybody is supposed to work together but differences and opinions get in the way, causing the guys and girls to form their groups. For the end-of-the-year prom, one side wants pasta and lace, the other wants sports and barbecue! The two groups square off but eventually work together, demonstrating the importance of cooperation and compromise.

Going to Guatemala

Dramedy. **High School.** 50-60 minutes. 11 actors. 6 males, 5 females.   ****A Latino-themed play****

A Latino student is chosen at the last minute to join a humanitarian group from his school that is headed to Guatemala. But since his Spanish is weak, he faces ridicule and criticism from certain peers. Jealousy and anger trickle throughout the campus as the trip approaches, and the social buzz of the high school becomes even more hectic when the student's trip money is stolen on campus, jeopardizing his trip.

Stravinsky's Kitchen

Comedy. **High School/College.** 12-15 minutes. 3 actors: 3 males (or females).

Two friends secretly enter the home of an employer to obtain a forgotten object but the homeowner abruptly arrives home while they are there. As they hide in the kitchen's pantry and plot their getaway, the two talk and eventually argue, exposing the true colors of one of them. Upon their hasty exit a mistake is made, and one of them capitalizes on this mistake, resulting in his/her fortune.

Forty Whacks

Drama. Spooky. **High School/College.** 25-35 minutes. 3 actors: 2 females, 1 male.

A pair of siblings have inherited the Lizzie Borden Bed and Breakfast in New England. Although the business was run for decades in a quiet, respectable fashion, one of the siblings is over-ambitious, wanting to unearth an alleged piece of buried evidence within the house. This brings about a chilly tension between brother and sister, and perhaps within the house itself.

John Calhoun and a Thief

Drama. **College.** 35-40 minutes. 3 actors: 2 females, 1 male.

Kicked out of a university PhD program, a bitter and dejected female lifts from the library archives original copies of John Calhoun's personal documents. Counseled and consoled by her roommates, her conscience slowly gets to her; but as she seeks entry to other universities her luck turns to worse, and the subsequent decisions she makes regarding the historic papers cause this one-act play to become darker, if not funnier.

Honoring the Hijacker

Drama. **College.** 12-15 minutes. 4 actors: 2 females, 2 males.

It's 1981, the ten-year anniversary of the famed hijacker D.B. Cooper. The play's four characters are attending a "D.B. Festival" and have stayed up very late, outlasting everybody else. The late night chit-chat goes from pranks and jokes to outright volatility, and suddenly this get-together becomes something that three of the four characters didn't bargain for.

It's a Super Day at Sammy's!

Comedy. **Middle or High School.** 35-40 minutes. 9 actors: 5 females, 4 males (4 possible adults).

Jodi has found a summer job at a travel agency. But her three younger siblings can't seem to live without her! They call her at the office incessantly, which interferes with the work. The standard telephone greeting "It's a super day at Sammy's!" becomes a repeated theme of this comedy, as Jodi struggles to reach a balance between her job and her nagging siblings

Three Tenners

Comedy/Drama. **Elementary through High School.** Three Ten-Minute Plays.

Three Creepy Plays

Drama. **Middle School through College.** Three short 'creepy' plays.

Hockey Masks in Hueytown

Drama. Spooky. **High School/College.** 20-25 minutes. 4 actors: 2 males, 2 females.

Driving home for Thanksgiving break, four college students stop off in a small rural town to retrieve one of the student's old family pictures. They reluctantly enter the empty home of his deceased uncle, a former producer for the Friday the 13th movies. Strange objects are found during their search . . but when a hockey mask surfaces, everything really goes sideways.

The Witch Makes Five

Drama. Spooky. **High School.** 10 minutes. 4 actors: 2 males, 2 females.

After a bizarre group camping trip, a student is checked into a youth mental facility . When she is visited by the other members of the trip, memories of the weekend trickle out . . . and horrific things begin to happen.

Mrs. Calapooza and the Culebra

Dramedy. **Grades 5-8.** 10 minutes. 5 actors: 3 females, 2 males.

Fed up with their grouchy teacher's classroom ways, four students complain and bicker back and forth during a Spanish quiz. The situation grows worse when the friends discover that one of them has pulled the ultimate prank on the teacher.

Raiders of the Lost Rakasa

Dramedy. **Grades 5-8.** 10 minutes. 7 actors: 4 females, 3 males.

Seven young explorers arrive at a cave in a far-off land in search of the great "Rakasa." They find what they want . . . along with a few of the cave's unexpected surprises.

www.ingramcontent.com/pod-product-compliance
Lightning Source LLC
Chambersburg PA
CBHW060538030426
42337CB00021B/4325